The Night Olympic Team

The Night Olympic Team

Fighting to Keep Drugs Out of the Games

Caroline Hatton

BOYDS MILLS PRESS

HONESDALE, PENNSYLVANIA

Contents

Introduction   9

1   One of the Biggest Doping Scandals in Olympic History   11

2   Will Cheaters Win?   15

3   A Troubled Past   19

4   Can the Scientists Find the New Drug?   23

5   Top Secret   29

6   Racing the Clock   33

7   In the Middle of the Night   37

8   Breaking News   41

9   The Endgame   45

Sports Smarts: Healthy Ways to Enhance Performance   48

Author's Note   49

Glossary   51

Resources   53

Index   55

Giant banners and tree lights adorned downtown Salt Lake City during the 2002 Olympic Winter Games.

Introduction

This book was written by a scientist, Dr. Caroline Hatton. She worked at the 2002 Winter Olympics, inside the lab that tested athletes for forbidden drugs. She didn't work with test tubes—only with brain power. After other scientists found drugs in athletes' samples, she checked that the results were correct. She asked, "How can we be sure?" in a hundred ways.

During a discussion among scientists in the lab, ideas flew around like sparks. A wave of excitement moved Caroline to decide that some day she would tell this story. She wanted to show young people science in action and that this difficult work was accomplished only because key people helped one another.

To write *The Night Olympic Team*, Caroline also interviewed those people—scientists, lawyers, and sports officials—and consulted more than eighty references. The book offers information about doping in sports to help readers make good decisions about drug use.

—*The Publisher*

The Olympic flame, 2002 Winter Olympics

1

One of the Biggest Doping Scandals in Olympic History

Night falls on the Olympic Village. Lights go out one by one. The Olympic flame bounces alone in the cold, the only movement till dawn.

Or is it?

Something's happening in the dark. In the snowy foothills above Salt Lake City, nowhere near the Olympic Village or event venues, car headlights stream into a parking lot, and mysterious figures file into a nearby building. More cars arrive through the night and in the wee hours of the morning.

These people are on the 2002 Winter Olympic Team. Dedicated to the Olympic dream, they've trained for years to get to the games. But their highest hope, shared with the entire world, is that their results won't make headlines.

It's not so bad. After all, even though they're not athletes, they're guaranteed to get the "gold" every night—at least that's how they like to think of it. Wouldn't you, if you were a scientist and your job was to test hundreds of bottles of golden urine from the world's best athletes at the biggest sporting event on earth?

Jeff Gorzek

Says scientist Jeff Gorzek, "I can't say I *like* working with urine. . . . But we test athletes to make sure they're not taking drugs that would give them an unfair advantage. I've competed in sports all my life and can imagine how I'd feel if I lost to a cheater."

Jeff is from Wisconsin, but his teammates are from Vietnam, Ukraine, France, and Germany. They're only five of forty scientists from the University of California at Los Angeles led by Professor Don Catlin, one of the world's top drug testers and a veteran of many Olympics. The forty scientists also include the author of this book.

Little does the team know that their work is about to expose one of the biggest doping scandals in Olympic history.

Night falls on Salt Lake City.

12

What Is Doping?

Taking drugs to enhance performance—to run faster, jump higher, be stronger—is called doping. Doping in sports is nothing new. More than two thousand years ago, a number of Greek athletes doped themselves at the ancient Olympics by eating bread soaked in opium (a painkiller), hoping to perform better. Modern-day Olympics ban doping because it's cheating and it can be bad for the athlete's health.

Most of the banned drugs are not illegal, as street drugs are. Many of the banned drugs have valid uses in treating disease. Some of the drugs require a prescription; others don't.

Banned drugs include stimulants, anabolic steroids, and blood boosters. Stimulants can make sprinters run faster, but they might also make athletes' hearts race or their bodies overheat. Anabolic steroids can make weightlifters stronger, but they might cause harm ranging from mild to life-threatening problems. Blood boosters make it possible to exercise longer before getting tired, but they might trigger strokes or heart attacks.

Do some athletes gulp down pills or get shots even though they're not sick and they know it's cheating? Yes! They're desperate to win. A gold medal might make an athlete a national hero or lead to fabulous wealth. Some athletes feel too much pressure to win from fans, loved ones, or even themselves.

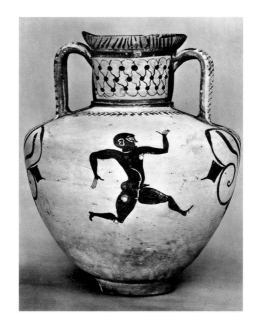

Ancient Greek vase depicting an Olympic athlete

Red blood cells carry oxygen.

2

Will Cheaters Win?

Some athletes, coaches, and trainers who are determined to cheat follow medical research as diligently as scientists. In long-distance sporting events, for example in cross-country skiing, speed skating, and cycling, they look for ways to keep athletes going, ways to boost endurance. They read about how red blood cells* carry oxygen to muscles and how healthy bodies make a hormone called EPO** (pronounced *ee-pee-oh*) that triggers red-cell production when needed.

Some illnesses cause people to have fewer red cells. Their muscles don't get enough oxygen, so they feel tired all the time. Giving them an artificial form of EPO called recombinant EPO boosts their red cells and restores their strength.

If healthy people take EPO, they can exercise longer before getting tired. So could athletes. But this is cheating. It might also kill the athletes because if they take too much, their thickened blood might clot in their brains. No

---

* Red blood cells are also called erythrocytes.
** EPO stands for erythropoietin, pronounced
ee-RIH-throw-PO-ee-tin.

Steven Elliott

respectable doctor would prescribe a blood booster except for acceptable medical reasons. But that never stopped cheaters from getting their hands on EPO and using it.

Boosting endurance by somehow increasing red cells is not a new idea. In fact, rumors of such attempts date back to the 1968 Summer Olympics in Mexico City.

Five months before the 2002 Winter Olympics, a new and improved blood-booster medicine, NESP* (pronounced *nesp*), became available. It was designed by a team led by Dr. Steven Elliott, a scientist at Amgen Corporation in Thousand Oaks, California.

The press began to contact Amgen about the possibility that athletes might use NESP to cheat by boosting endurance—a dark side of NESP that Steve hadn't foreseen. During the years of hard work it took to create the new medicine, all Steve had ever had in mind was to help people with illnesses such as kidney disease or cancer. So when he heard the alien notion that NESP could be abused by some athletes, he was deeply annoyed.

"How dare they?" he remembers saying before turning speechless with indignation.

* NESP stands for novel erythropoietic (red-blood-cell-production) stimulating protein. It is also called darbepoetin (pronounced DAR-bee-PO-ee-tin) alfa or Aranesp.

Endurance athletes knew they would be tested at the 2002 Olympics. But because NESP was so new, no one could imagine that the Olympic Lab scientists would figure out how to test for it in time for the Games. Experts outside the lab expected cheaters to use NESP and get away with it. And that's what the whole world thought, as athletes moved into the Olympic Village.

EPO: The Body's Blood-Boosting Hormone

When the body needs more oxygen, it tells the kidneys to make EPO. EPO makes new red blood cells grow, and they carry oxygen to all parts of the body.

Some illnesses cause people to have fewer red cells. Their muscles don't get enough oxygen, so they feel tired all the time. For example, in some types of kidney disease, the kidneys don't make enough EPO. Another example involves cancer patients who receive "chemo" (pronounced KEY-mo), short for chemotherapy, or treatment with chemicals to kill cancer cells. But medicines have many effects, some wanted, some not. Chemo tends to kill all fast-growing cells, not only bad cancer cells but also good cells, such as hair cells (that's why hair can fall out during chemo) and new red blood cells in the bone marrow.

Giving hope for relief to such patients, Amgen started making recombinant human EPO by recombinant DNA* technology, a way of cutting and pasting together DNA bits called genes. The gene that is the code for EPO is pasted into the DNA of a special cell in a lab dish. This EPO gene tells the cell to make EPO—in other words, it turns this cell into an EPO factory. EPO oozes out of the cell, into the liquid where the cell is kept. Next, when this cell divides into two new cells, both cells make EPO. When these two cells divide and become four new cells, all four cells make EPO. After many divisions, a gazillion cells all make EPO—enough to collect and prepare for use as a medicine. It took years to figure out how to make EPO.

EPO became available as a blood-booster medicine in 1989. EPO shots can make patients who are so weak that they can hardly get out of bed feel full of life again.

* *DNA stands for <u>d</u>eoxyribo<u>n</u>ucleic (pronounced dee-OX-ee-RYE-bow-new-CLAY-ik) <u>a</u>cid. See box on page 31 for details.*

The 1984 Summer Olympics in Los Angeles

3

A Troubled Past

As athletes moved into the Olympic Village, sports officials, reporters, tourists . . . and the UCLA Olympic Lab scientists checked into their hotel rooms. Several of these scientists had worked at the Olympics before, at the 1984 Games in Los Angeles and 1996 Games in Atlanta.

During each of those Games, they had worked day and night. They had found banned drugs in athletes' urine samples. They had reported these results to the International Olympic Committee.

The scientists knew the samples only by code numbers—no names, no countries. Only the International Olympic Committee knew who had given each sample. Athletes who tested positive for banned drugs had to give back their medals. But in a few of the cases reported by the lab, the committee never identified or punished the athletes. Ten years after the 1984 Games, reporters discovered that official papers had been shredded accidentally before bottle numbers could be linked to athletes' names. And three months after the 1996 Games, the media revealed that nothing had been done about a few drug cases, because the Olympic committee had "scientific doubts" about a kind of test it had required. The names of the athletes remain unknown to this day.

For the scientists who work so hard to catch cheaters, it's hard to see the athletes get away with it.

Fortunately, every sport drug-testing program is different. Some are better than others at policing drug abuse. In the best programs, the rules of science and sports are followed, fair and square.

Would the rules be followed at the 2002 Olympics in Salt Lake City?

Don Catlin

The UCLA* Olympic Lab was founded by Don Catlin, a medical doctor. How does a regular doctor turn into a science sleuth, outwitting international sports cheats?

The first time Don remembers paying attention to doping in sports was in 1982. As a professor at the UCLA School of Medicine, he was asked if he would be interested in opening a lab to run the doping-control tests for the 1984 Olympic Summer Games in Los Angeles.

When he studied the list of banned drugs, he didn't recognize half the names. Some were foreign. Others had long been abandoned in medicine. There were too many.

"This can't be done," said Don.

Besides, the whole notion of doping in sports made no sense to him. Why would a young, healthy, elite athlete take drugs?

Don went to the library and read everything he could find about the subject. It didn't take long because there wasn't much. Next, he visited world-class experts to tap their experience and wisdom.

He also went to the local gym to ask questions and learn everything he could about the abuse of steroids and other performance-enhancing drugs in sports. He couldn't believe the risks that some young people were taking with their health and perhaps their lives.

Something had to be done. He was hooked! But could he make a difference?

To find out, Don started a lab after all, the UCLA Olympic Lab, in 1982. To focus his efforts, he quit seeing patients. He ended up doing what he first thought was impossible, testing Olympic athletes. Ever since then, he has devoted his work life to fighting drugs in sports.

His lab grew to be the largest of its kind in the world. It is accredited (approved)

Yvonne Chambers receives samples.

by the World Anti-Doping Agency. The lab conducts drug tests for the U.S. Olympic Committee, National Collegiate Athletic Association (NCAA), National Football League (NFL), and Minor League Baseball.

When the Olympics are held in another country, that country's lab tests the Games. But the UCLA Olympic Lab tests all U.S. athletes who compete in the U.S. Olympic Trials—whether or not they make the Olympic team. The lab staff works hard every day, testing athletes' urine samples, doing research, and publishing results to stamp out the abuse of one drug after another.

What does it take to work there as a scientist? A college degree in science, such as chemistry, biochemistry, or biology is necessary. And to rise to the level of responsibility where a scientist can decide that a sample contains a banned drug, it is best to have a Ph.D.—a doctoral degree in science.

After twenty-five years as the lab director, Don Catlin resigned in 2007 to devote all his time and energy to Anti-Doping Research, Inc., a new institute that he founded. The UCLA Olympic Lab continued under new management.

The 2002 Olympics opening ceremony

4

Can the Scientists Find the New Drug?

The 2002 Winter Games began, complete with souvenir pins, T-shirts, and medal ceremonies. The first thing an athlete might hear when crossing the finish line—or anytime while at the Olympics—is, "Lucky you! You get to give urine for a drug test."*

When that happens, the athlete goes into the rest room with a plastic cup to . . . um, fill. How do officials know that real urine from the right person goes into the cup? They watch. Yes, they go into the stall and stare. Talk about getting to meet athletes! But these officials are not the scientists who test urine at the lab, where Olympic athletes never go.

How can athletes put up with stares while urinating? Because if they want to play, those are the rules. And they know if everyone is watched, no one can cheat. Thank goodness only men observe men, and only women observe women.

The urine goes from the cup into bottles, into a box, into a bag, into a van, and off to the lab. By then it's nighttime—time for the lab team to get to work. Testing can't wait until morning because the Olympics can't wait. Some athletes compete more than once. Those who broke the rules by using banned drugs must be removed from competition as soon as possible.

* At the 2002 Winter Olympics, blood samples were also taken from some athletes for testing.

French scientist Françoise Lasne (above) led the team that invented the EPO test. Henry Truong (left) sets up an electrical device for testing.

To avoid mix-ups, urine is measured into labeled test tubes one bottle at a time. Of the forty lab-team members at the 2002 Olympics, some tested samples for stimulants. Others looked for anabolic steroids or other drugs. Five looked for blood boosters. Jeff Gorzek was one of the five.

The EPO test he ran had been perfected by a French scientist, Dr. Françoise Lasne (pronounced *fran-swahz lahn*), and her teammates to detect recombinant EPO. The question was, could the old test for recombinant EPO detect the new NESP?

Wearing a white lab coat and rubber gloves, Jeff took samples through dozens of steps. He stirred, spun, and heated them. Then he passed them to a teammate on the next shift. Now came the most amazing step: isoelectric focusing, also called "running a gel."

To see if the test can tell apart natural EPO, recombinant EPO, and the new NESP, the scientists worked with a true, known sample of each. Each one is a mix of several forms containing the same protein with different sugars attached. The samples were put on a thin layer of gel. Electricity was run through it, and—voilà!—the protein forms spread out. Not only that, but the natural EPO, recombinant EPO, and NESP spread out in completely different,

Inna Tregub prepares a gel for testing.

Andreas Breidbach prepares Olympic athletes' urine samples for testing.

telltale patterns. Best of all, no new test was needed to detect NESP because the old test could detect the new drug just fine.

The outside world still believed that the lab had no test for NESP. The Olympics zoomed along. The scientists kept testing. And one night, something phenomenal happened.

The "B" Sample in Sports Drug Testing

An athlete who is tested for drugs must urinate into a plastic cup while an official watches to make sure that the sample is real urine from the correct person. Next, the athlete chooses a pair of bottles from several that are labeled only with numbers and letters, for example, 1234567A and 1234567B—no name, no country. The sample is split—some poured into the "A" bottle, some into the "B" bottle. The athlete watches as both bottles are sealed. Both bottles go to the lab.

At first the lab opens only the "A" bottle, takes out a portion of urine and screens it—looks for all banned drugs. If a drug is found, the finding must be confirmed. The number on the "A" bottle is checked, the bottle is opened again, and a fresh portion of urine is tested for the drug. Only after the drug has been found in this second portion of urine from the "A" bottle does the lab report which drug was found and in which sample number.

The athlete or the athlete's representative has the right to come to the lab and examine the "B" sample, which is still sealed, intact, exactly as the athlete last saw it. Then the athlete or representative can watch as the "B" bottle is opened, a portion of urine is taken out, and the test is repeated once more to confirm that the drug can be found for the third time.

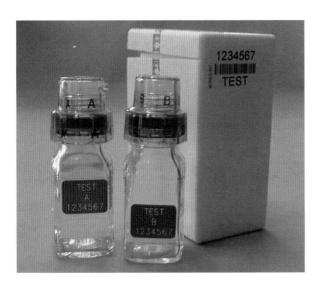

Each urine sample is split—some poured into the "A" bottle, and some into the "B" bottle.

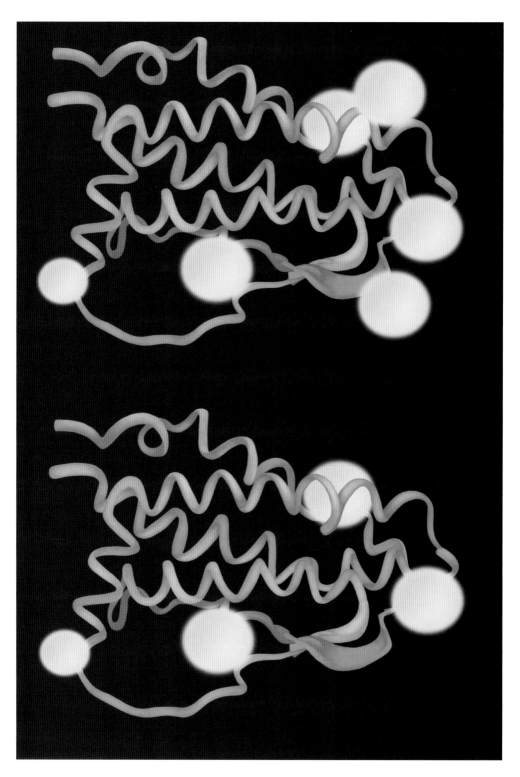

An artist's vision of NESP and recombinant EPO. Each molecule is a protein (ribbon) with sugars attached where the balls are shown. NESP has two more sugars than recombinant EPO.

5

Top Secret

One night, something phenomenal happened at the lab. The scientists found the new drug, NESP, in an athlete's urine. Later, they found it in more samples. They had no idea whom they had caught, because all they had were bottle code numbers—no names, no countries. Only the International Olympic Committee knew who had given each urine sample.

Positive results are top secret. Reporting them is a serious matter. It might end the sports career and smash the dreams of someone who's dedicated an entire life to this quest. In hushed meetings behind closed doors, the scientists checked findings and bottle numbers.

Some athletes accused of doping challenge the findings and hire lawyers to defend them. Legal fights go on for years. Athletes' lawyers attack lab work, paperwork, sports rules—trying to show that they're no good. Lab scientists do their best to foresee lawyers' complaints and craft answers in advance. Then they are prepared to convince sports officials, athletes, and lawyers that a banned drug was indeed present.

Before reporting a positive, lab director Don Catlin wanted to be absolutely certain that the test results were correct. Because NESP had never been reported before, he consulted his best scientists for days and nights. He asked them as well as lawyers, with more than a hundred years of experience among them, to help pile up scientific proof. They pooled their knowledge, ideas, and strengths.

When Don spoke on his cell phone, his lab partners constantly reminded him to use obscure terms to avoid revealing anything about the secret cases because cell phone conversations can be heard by outsiders. Some days, Don took a teammate for a drive beyond the last buildings on the fringes of Salt Lake City, into the wilderness, to talk privately where no one could hear them.

The single most important action Don took was to call the best-qualified man in the world to identify NESP: its inventor, Steve Elliott.

Don Catlin and the author discussed test results and their possible ramifications in the wilderness, where no one could hear them.

Making Mutants: Using Recombinant DNA Technology to Create a Supermedicine

DNA is found in cells. It contains all the information needed to make a living thing. It determines whether that thing will be a mushroom, an elephant, or a human being. DNA is passed from parents to children.

DNA is made of bits called genes. Genes are codes for eye color, hair curliness, and many other details. Some genes are codes that tell cells to make particular proteins. Some proteins are hormones the body needs to function properly. One example is EPO, the body's blood booster.

EPO is a protein with sugars attached. Studies on EPO had shown that the more sugars on the protein backbone, the better it worked. Logically, Amgen scientist Steve Elliott set out to put as many sugars as he could fit on EPO.

To make room for more sugars, first he and his team had to make small changes to the protein backbone. To do that, they had to tweak the EPO gene in the DNA. Such a change in the DNA is called a mutation. That's why the molecules they made are called EPO mutants. One step at a time, taking weeks from start to finish, they made hundreds and hundreds of mutants. Some mutants didn't work, but some worked better than natural EPO.

One mutant worked especially well. Steve had created a supermedicine, NESP. It lasted longer in the body. And that made it possible for a patient who needed several shots of EPO a week to get fewer shots—maybe only one a week—of NESP instead.

How big a deal could it be? A handyman working at Steve's home helped him understand. The man said his mother had cancer. She was awfully sick and had to ride a long way to the doctor's office to get an EPO shot three times a week. A medicine needed only once a week would bring her enormous relief.

Giant banner in downtown Salt Lake City

6

Racing the Clock

NESP inventor Steve Elliott was attending a science conference in Louisiana when his cell phone rang.

"Read your e-mail," said Don's unmistakable, low-rumbling voice. "I sent you images I want you to see. Tell me what you think."

From experience, Steve knew how images showed results from the French test for EPO—different, telltale patterns for natural and recombinant EPO. He rushed to his hotel room and plugged in his laptop. He saw a new, striking pattern where the lab scientists had run the test on NESP itself. And he saw a pattern labeled only with a mysterious code number, and that pattern matched the pattern of NESP.

"Wow!" he said to Don. "That's it. That's NESP."

Don asked Steve to write a letter to the International Olympic Committee describing what he saw in the images—as soon as possible, please, this was an emergency! In his hotel room, Steve pushed himself, racing the clock. He was about to get involved in a very serious matter: accusing athletes of doping themselves with the medicine that Amgen makes to help sick people. Steve knew the responsible thing to do was to seek approval from the Amgen lawyers in California. The problem was, it was 4:00 p.m. there on a Friday, and Don couldn't wait.

Steve grabbed the phone. He called the top lawyer at Amgen, only to find out that he was away and couldn't be reached. Same luck with the second person he tried. The third Amgen lawyer was at home with a nasty case of the flu. A legal assistant came to the rescue by e-mailing the letter to the sick lawyer, then calling him at home later. They went over what was happening as well as the letter that Steve had prepared to send to Don. The approval was e-mailed to Steve. Steve e-mailed the letter to Don. Don gave it to the Olympic Committee, barely in time for a hearing. It was around midnight, the night before the closing ceremony.

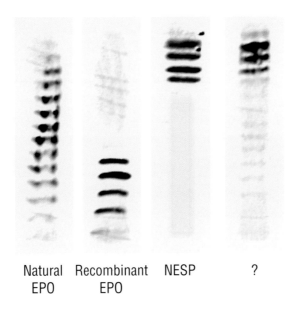

Natural Recombinant NESP   ?
EPO   EPO

Test your cheat-busting skills. If you were a scientist reading a gel, could you find a match by comparing patterns between the mystery substance and the three known substances?

What Are Anabolic Steroids?

Taking anabolic steroids is especially dangerous for young people. Anabolic steroids are hormones, or chemicals that regulate bodily functions. One anabolic steroid naturally made by the body is testosterone, which turns boys into men by triggering changes such as the growth of body hair, muscles, and reproductive organs. Synthetic (artificial) steroids mimic testosterone. Anabolic steroids can make an athlete bigger and stronger. They are the banned drugs that are most talked about in sports.

Anabolic steroids and blood boosters like EPO are two completely different kinds of hormones. Anabolic steroids should also not be confused with corticosteroids, which are used as medicines to treat asthma and inflammation. On rare occasions, doctors prescribe anabolic steroids to medical patients with serious illnesses such as cancer or AIDS. In fact, getting anabolic steroids without a doctor's prescription is illegal in the United States.

An even stronger reason why it's a bad idea for healthy young people to take anabolic steroids is that serious medical problems can arise. Possible complications—"side effects"—range from mild to life-threatening: acne is common, girls might grow mustaches, boys might grow breasts. Some users get angry while on the drugs, depressed when they stop taking them. And even if they quit taking steroids, young people might stop growing taller—for good.

But what about sports stars who take them? For example, Kelli White was the fastest woman in the world in 2003. She won gold medals in the 100-meter and 200-meter races at the World Track & Field Championships. She has since confessed that during that year, she used a stimulant (for which she was caught), as well as an anabolic steroid and the blood booster EPO. She has now lost all her medals and world records. "I made a choice that I will forever regret," she said. "The choice to compete clean is always the best choice."

And a Texas boy who loved sports, Chris Wash, will tell you about his experience after he began taking steroids at age fifteen, and why he will never touch them again. The steroid-related suicide of a friend was his wake-up call to stop. Side effects still made Chris's life miserable more than a year after he stopped taking the drugs. They held him back from going to college and playing basketball. In his own words, "They messed up my life."

Downtown Salt Lake City during the 2002 Olympics

7

In the Middle of the Night

After double-checking test results for days and nights, lab director Don Catlin reported the NESP findings to the International Olympic Committee. He provided Steve's letter to convince Dr. Jacques Rogge (pronounced *zhahk roe-g*), the top Olympic official, that NESP was indeed the drug that had been found in the urine samples. The purpose of the letter was to give Jacques the confidence to accuse athletes of doping themselves with a new medicine that had never been reported in sports.

That's how much work it took to build strong cases from step one. "What did it," Don later recalled, "is that Jacques Rogge agreed to proceed."

At the time, Jacques was the new president of the International Olympic Committee. He was perhaps the biggest sports big shot in the world. He knew that in the opinions of many people, drug cases are bad news, likely to lead to disqualifications and to throw the shadow of scandal on the Olympics.

In an interview long after the Games, Jacques remembered, "I was advised that the lab had found suspect cases and I was asked what to do. And

Jacques Rogge

I said, 'Well, we go ahead full steam.' I was told that some big nations were involved and it would be a noisy issue. I said, 'I don't care. This is something that we have to pursue.' And that's what I did."

And Don told a reporter about Jacques, "He's a no-nonsense person who understands the role of drugs in sports intimately, and he's not afraid of it."

On the last Saturday night of the Games, the Olympic Committee held a closed hearing on one of the cases to get all sides of the story, including the athlete's, before deciding whether to take away any medals. Don Catlin spent half the night outside the door of the hearing room in case he was needed to answer science questions. He was asked to go into the room for a few minutes. Then he was allowed to leave.

What would the committee decide?

Science Sleuths Solve Mystery

Detecting banned drugs in athletes has become a constant battle for sports officials and lab scientists. The work is becoming even more difficult with "designer" drugs such as THG,* an anabolic steroid that was designed to be undetectable by existing urine tests.

Anabolic steroids such as testosterone are the natural male hormones that trigger the changes of puberty in boys such as the growth of a beard, muscles, and reproductive organs. Athletes who take them to get big and strong risk dangerous side effects. Young people risk stunting their growth—even if they stop taking the drugs.

The THG saga began with a clandestine used syringe. It was sent to U.S. anti-doping officials in 2003 by an anonymous coach. He said the syringe had contained a secret steroid used by some athletes to cheat and not get caught.

The officials sent clear drops from the syringe to their chemistry sleuths, lab director Don Catlin and his team at UCLA. Their mission: to crack this latest doping mystery. They used chromatography to separate the chemicals in the sample. Then mass spectrometry was used to help the chemists match the sample's molecular fingerprint with known molecular fingerprints. No luck; the mystery compound—X—didn't match any compound they knew.

The chemists looked instead to parts of the molecular fingerprint. If they could match parts of it, they would have a few pieces of a chemical jigsaw puzzle. Based on many comparisons, they drew pieces of the puzzle on paper.

Then they put the puzzle together and drew on paper their best guess for X. They called it tetrahydrogestrinone, or THG for short. It looked to the scientists as if the crooked chemists had added four hydrogen atoms to the steroid gestrinone. Since there was no ready-made THG to match with X, Don and his team made their own THG. They had a match! "Bingo!" said Don.

Once the designer drug was identified, it took weeks to invent a new urine test for it. Before the discovery of THG, cheaters had been caught only on medicinal steroids. THG is a big deal because it's not a medicine. It was made only to beat the test. It shows how far crooks will go—but they can go no further with THG because Don Catlin has told all anti-doping labs worldwide how to test for it. Anyone using it now can be busted.

---

*THG stands for tetrahydrogestrinone.

The 2002 Olympics closing ceremony

8

Breaking News

The NESP cases had been reported to the International Olympic Committee. The scientists wondered how long it would take, after these Olympics, for the world to know the truth. The only way for the scientists to find out whether the committee had decided to disqualify athletes and take away medals was by watching TV like everyone else.

On Sunday afternoon, a few hours before the closing ceremony, CNN announced breaking news about Olympic athletes caught using NESP. In an instant, eighteen years of doubt and darkness since the lost positive cases of 1984 and 1996 were erased forever. For the scientists, nights and days of toil, all these years of not giving up, suddenly became worth every hardship.

On Monday morning at the lab, some of the EPO-test team members shook hands. The world knew about the athletes who broke the rules. No matter what happened in court, the scientists had done their job. They wanted to protect one another from the possible heartbreak of losing the cases in court some day for all the wrong reasons, and knowing drug users got away.

The *Los Angeles Times* called it "a breathtaking scandal infecting the sport and staining the final day of the 19th Winter Olympics." How did Jeff, the lab scientist, feel about spoiling the party? "Proud! That may sound funny that I'm happy we took away athletes' medals. But they were cheating. We awarded medals to the true winners—those who won *without* drugs."

All three athletes were cross-country skiers—two Russian women, Larissa Lazutina and Olga Danilova, and one German man turned Spanish citizen, Johann Muehlegg. Three athletes out of the more than 2,400 competing in the 2002 Winter Olympics. Three who had won a total of eight medals, some of them prior to getting caught for using NESP. Muehlegg and Lazutina each lost one gold medal. All three were suspended from competing for two years, a long time in a top athlete's career.

Thus the International Olympic Committee took action against every athlete who had tested positive for NESP. It also took action against each individual who had tested positive for other banned drugs at the 2002 Winter Games.

The end, right? Wrong!

Salt Lake City at nightfall with the Olympic rings lit up on the mountainside

Can Athletes Be Thrown Out for Taking Cold Medicine?

Let's say an athlete has a cold and takes medicine to breathe better. Many such medicines contain pseudoephedrine (pronounced SUE-doe-eh-FED-rin) as the active ingredient. It is a decongestant, which means that it clears your stuffy nose. But like most medicines, it has many different effects, some wanted, some not. One side effect is that pseudoephedrine is also a stimulant. It might perk you up and make you feel like a champ. It might let you run faster for a longer time. It might also make your heart race and your body overheat, not to mention that it could get you so excited that you might do something that would hurt yourself or others.

Years ago, pseudoephedrine was banned from sports. But if an athlete was caught on it and chose to plead for forgiveness, claiming that he or she had a cold and didn't know any better, some sports organizations would let the athlete go. Inadvertent use was excused.

As time passed, sports organizations were faced with the reality that they couldn't tell honest mistakes from lies. Athletes determined to cheat might dope themselves with pseudoephedrine, then pretend they had a cold and didn't know any better.

By the 2000 Olympics in Sydney, the International Olympic Committee had tightened the rules and moved toward strict liability. Strict liability means that the rules are the rules—it doesn't matter how the drug got into your urine sample. If the drug is there, you can't play.

At the 2000 Olympics, Romanian gymnast Andreea Raducan won the all-around gold, but her urine test revealed the presence of pseudoephedrine. She explained that she had had a cold and that her team doctor had given her the medication. The International Olympic Committee believed her and felt bad for her, but they applied strict liability—no excuses. They did not take back her other medal or kick her out of the Olympics. They imposed on her the lightest sanction that the rules allowed by taking away only her gold medal. She filed an appeal, but the court denied it.

By the 2004 Olympics in Athens, the responsibility for maintaining the list of banned drugs was given by the International Olympic Committee to a new organization, the World Anti-Doping Agency (WADA). WADA decided to remove pseudoephedrine from the list. Many other drugs remain on the banned list, however, and WADA adds new ones every year.

Will drug-free athletes such as Canada's Beckie Scott win?

9

The Endgame

The International Olympic Committee punished the three athletes who tested positive for NESP. But the story was not over. The accused athletes protested. They appealed the rulings. They hired international teams of lawyers. The International Olympic Committee's lawyers, Jan Paulsson and Zachary Douglas, who lived and worked in Paris, braced themselves for the court battle.

The first thing lawyers do is get the facts. Jan "handed over a few piles" of papers for Zac to read. Zac devoured the bundles, three to be exact: sports anti-doping rules, lab documents, and pure science articles.

The NESP cases would be won or lost based on scientific evidence. Zac had studied science as a schoolboy, but that was a long time ago and it was not his strongest subject. Fortunately, Don Catlin, the lab director, was used to teaching science to lawyers.

Scientist and lawyer worked together, on the phone for hours, day after day, over many months. Zac the lawyer articulated legal arguments he wanted

Clean athlete Beckie Scott gets the gold, which she had deserved all along.

to make to win the cases. Don the scientist explained the science behind the arguments.

Zac did his level best to make the legal arguments as strong as Don's science work. Zac knew that if the International Olympic Committee lost the cases, "Dr. Catlin's heroic efforts to catch the cheats would be in vain," he said in a later interview. "He had come to trust me. I was not going to let him down."

Next Jan, the senior lawyer, made the key points as convincing as possible. Lawyers for both sides filed legal writings the size of novels with the court.

Zac prepared Don Catlin and NESP inventor Steve Elliott to testify in court. Zac was thrilled to work with two world leaders in science.

The two Russian women and the Spanish man who tested positive for NESP got two separate court dates nearly a year after the Olympics. Don Catlin and Steve Elliott flew to Switzerland to testify.

All three cases turned out the same way. After the court lawyers heard both sides, everyone went home. Some days later, the court lawyers reached a decision. They denied the appeals. They also ordered the athletes to return the medals they had won in the events in which they were caught using NESP.

Another year later, after more court battles, the athletes were ordered to give back the rest of their medals. When punished athletes lose medals, the athletes who came in behind them get bumped up. For example, in one event, after Lazutina lost her gold medal and Danilova

The lab's legal documents for the three athletes' cases

lost her silver medal, the bronze medalist finally won the gold, which she had deserved all along. This drug-free athlete was Beckie Scott* of Canada.

The whole world could see that NESP users can't win. This victory helped put an end to the abuse of NESP in sports.

The night Olympic team is like a group of custodians—keepers of a key Olympic ideal. Without them, nothing would stop cheaters from taking drugs to get an edge. Honest athletes, even if they don't want to take drugs, might believe that they have to if they ever want to win. Fortunately for them, scientists, sports leaders, and lawyers team up worldwide to protect their freedom to compete without drugs.

What If an Athlete Needs a Banned Medicine?

Many sports organizations allow athletes and their doctors to ask for permission to use a medicine that is on the banned list. For example, steroids are banned. But if athletes need to use an asthma inhaler that contains a corticosteroid, they can ask for permission to use it.

This kind of permission is called Therapeutic Use Exemption, or TUE. The athlete must fill out a form and provide a doctor's note. The sports organization asks a group of doctors (other than the athlete's doctor) to decide whether to give permission or to deny it.

How do the doctors decide? They follow the rules and ask three questions:

- *Would the athlete have serious health problems if he or she didn't take the drug?*
- *Would the amount of drug needed to treat the illness help the athlete perform better in the sport competition?*
- *Is there no other drug that can help the health problem?*

If a TUE is granted, the athlete should mention it when he or she gives a urine sample for drug testing. When the lab finds the drug and reports it, the sports organization matches the bottle number with the athlete's name and the TUE, and records the test result as negative.

If a TUE is denied, the doctors must explain why. The athlete can appeal, and a court makes the final decision.

* Beckie Scott was appointed to the World Anti-Doping Agency Athlete Committee in March 2005, three years after the Salt Lake City Olympics.

Sports Smarts: Healthy Ways to Enhance Performance

Get enough sleep

You snooze, you win! If you are well rested, you won't be groggy or cranky. You'll play your favorite sport better.

Tap the power of water

Drink plenty of water before, during, and after playing a sport.

Eat like a champ

Eat healthy foods, such as fresh fruit for snacks.
Stop eating when you're full.

Use top tips for tip-top shape

Turn off the TV. Walk away from the computer.
Move! Play outside, dance, jump rope, walk, bike, swim. . . . Do sit-ups, push-ups, jumping jacks. . . .
Being fit will make you better at any sport.

Work on your skills

No matter what sport you love best, you probably need special skills such as dribbling a ball or correct swimming strokes. Work on your skills, little by little—getting better takes time.

Expect bad days

Everybody has good days and bad days, even champions. Don't let bad days get you down. Look forward to more good days.

Author's Note

Advances in doping in sports reflect or anticipate advances in medicine and challenge drug testers to keep up. In some cases, such as that of the oxygenation medicine RSR-13, testers began testing for the drug as rumors surfaced about its abuse in sports long before it reached the market. For designer steroids made only to beat the test, testers were one step behind (with norbolethone in 2002) or ahead (with THG in 2003 and madol, also known as DMT, in 2004). Human growth hormone has long been abused, but whether there is a test for it is the subject of some debate and confusion as of December 2007. And some believe that gene doping (using genes or cells), for which there is no test yet, is looming.

Although the media often describes anti-doping efforts as an endless game of cat-and-mouse, a look at previous decades shows tremendous progress. Sports organizations add drugs to their prohibited list far quicker than in the past. Harmonization of sports rules (prohibited drugs, sanctions) across different sports organizations and of lab tests across different labs, as well as the collaboration among world sports and drug-enforcement bodies, has vastly improved. Investigations and confessions expose doping further back in time. Research funding for scientists to invent new tests is slowly increasing. The system is not perfect, but it is capable of changing, mostly for the better.

An ongoing debate simmers about whether performance-enhancing drugs should be allowed in sports. Some say they should be, especially in a pill-popping, tummy-tucking society where it is acceptable to use medicine to make healthy people better. Others say that sports would become a competition between pharmacologists, that giving drug use a free rein would open the door to serious toxicity when risk-taking athletes push the envelope, and that athletes would, more than ever, feel coerced to dope in order to remain competitive. In a curious dichotomy, perhaps the only area where there is no doubt or controversy is when it comes to young people: these drugs, especially anabolic steroids, are unanimously considered harmful to the young. Anabolic steroids and youth often make news in the United States.

The U.S. government is growing more concerned, as shown by some milestones in legislation:
- The Steroid Control Act of 1990 made anabolic steroids controlled substances.
- DSHEA (pronounced *duh-shay*), the Dietary Supplement Health and Education Act of 1994, was supposed to help lower health-care costs by giving the American public access to over-the-counter health products. It allowed the sale of dietary supplements without proof of safety or efficacy as long as they were natural products and manufacturers didn't claim that they helped diagnose, cure, or prevent disease. However, these supplements included anabolic-steroid prohormones—chemicals such as "andro" that by definition are converted by the body into male hormones. American consumers were

testing their safety and efficacy by taking them at their own risk—paying to serve as lab rats.

- The Steroid Control Act of 2004 closed the DSHEA loophole for virtually all anabolic steroid prohormones by making them controlled substances that can no longer legally be sold over the counter.

As more kids try anabolic steroids at younger ages and as steroid-related teen suicides and confessions of steroid use by high-school football players appear in the news, some states have passed legislation to require steroid education in schools or to conduct mandatory drug testing for steroids, which is expensive.

Keeping his eye on the future, Don Catlin wonders if it might be possible to turn the culture around and reward honest athletes instead of punishing cheaters. If athletes volunteered to show that they're drug-free, he would like them to get free medical care and free advice on nutrition and fitness. Their names would be published. They would agree to be tested for banned drugs at any time. Don would also monitor biomarkers such as serum hormones or blood pressure. If lab readings are stable, great. If they start shifting and the athlete, together with trusted physicians, can't come up with any explanation that doesn't involve drugs, the athlete would not be suspended from sports but merely dropped from the program, and the information would be made public. Although other programs by different anti-doping organizations around the world are beginning to monitor athletes in this fashion, Don's program differs in two ways: it has rewards and no sanctions—it's all carrots and no sticks. This Volunteer Program is what Don wants to try, to get drugs and cheating under control, and save the soul of sports. He says that if sports can make this program work, it will reduce legal, technology, and overall costs. So who wants to fund it?

Glossary

anabolic steroid any of several male hormones. In normal male development, natural anabolic steroids trigger the changes such as the deepening of the voice and growth of reproductive organs that lead to puberty and manhood. Artificial anabolic steroids are used to treat rare diseases. Some athletes use these drugs to develop bigger, stronger muscles. But the drugs might also cause harm ranging from mild to life-threatening problems, including acne, mood swings, depression when users quit the drugs, or stopping young people from ever growing taller.

biomarker a biological marker, indication, or reading such as weight or blood pressure.

chromatography a lab technique used by scientists to separate the chemicals in samples.

corticosteroid any of several medicines used to treat asthma or inflammation; not to be confused with anabolic steroids.

designer drug in sports, a drug that is created and produced illegally for the purpose of escaping detection by tests.

doping taking drugs to enhance performance—to run faster, jump higher, be stronger, etc.

EPO (erythropoietin) a hormone that triggers red-blood-cell production.

hormone a chemical made by the body to regulate bodily functions.

IOC (International Olympic Committee) the group that organizes the Olympic Summer and Winter Games, Youth Olympic Games, and Paralympic Games.

mass spectrometry a lab technique used by scientists to identify the chemicals in samples.

NESP (novel erythropoietic stimulating protein) a medicine that boosts production of red blood cells. Also called darbepoetin alfa or Aranesp.

pseudoephedrine a medicine used to clear stuffy noses or congestion. Some athletes use the drug for its side effect as a stimulant.

recombinant DNA technology a way of cutting and pasting (recombining) DNA bits (genes) inside living cells.

recombinant EPO an artificial form of EPO made through recombinant DNA technology and used to treat patients whose bodies do not make enough red blood cells.

stimulant a medicine that increases alertness. Some athletes use stimulants to delay feeling tired, but the drugs might also make the heart race or the body overheat.

strict liability in anti-doping, a principle used when an athlete's sample contains a prohibited drug. *Strict liability* means that such an athlete is considered to have broken the rules even if it wasn't his or her fault. In that case, lighter sanctions are possible.

testosterone the main natural anabolic steroid.

THG (tetrahydrogestrinone) a designer anabolic steroid used only to cheat.

toxicity the quality that makes a chemical, such as a poison, harm life forms (for example, plants, animals, or humans) by making them sick or killing them.

TUE (Therapeutic Use Exemption) official permission given to an athlete to use a prohibited medicine.

WADA (World Anti-Doping Agency) an organization that fights against doping in sports.

Resources

YOUNG READERS

GENERAL

Books

Galas, Judith. *Drugs and Sports*. San Diego: Lucent Books, 1997.

Santella, Thomas M. *Body Enhancement Products*. Philadelphia: Chelsea House, 2005.

ANABOLIC STEROIDS

Web Site*

U.S. Department of Health and Human Services and SAMHSA's National Clearinghouse for Alcohol and Drug Information. "Tips for Teens: The Truth About Steroids." ncadi.samhsa.gov/govpubs/phd726

Article

Wash, Chris, and Ellen Labrecque. "Steroids Messed Up My Life." *Sports Illustrated for Kids*, October 2004, 52.

Book

Adams, Jacqueline. *Steroids*. San Diego: Lucent Books, 2006.

CHILDREN'S HEALTH AND FITNESS

Web Sites

The Nemours Foundation's Center for Children's Health Media.
TeensHealth. kidshealth.org/teen
KidsHealth for Kids. kidshealth.org/kid

ADULTS

GENERAL

Anti-Doping Organizations and Web Sites
National Center for Drug Free Sport, Inc. (NCDFS). www.drugfreesport.com

United States Anti-Doping Agency (USADA). www.usantidoping.org

World Anti-Doping Agency (WADA). www.wada-ama.org

Article

Alexander, Brian. "The Awful Truth About Drugs in Sports." *Outside*, July 2005, 100–108. outside.away.com/outside

Book

Callahan, David. *The Cheating Culture: Why More Americans Are Doing Wrong to Get Ahead*. New York: Harcourt, 2004. www.cheatingculture.com

Documentary

Australian Broadcasting Corporation. *Dope: The Battle for the Soul of Sport*. 2004.
DVD (or VHS) and study guide available from www.enhancetv.com.au

ANABOLIC STEROIDS

Web Site

MayoClinic.com. www.mayoclinic.com
Search for "anabolic steroids."

Articles

Adler, Jerry. "Toxic Strength." *Newsweek*, December 20, 2004, 44–52.

Starr, Mark. "Play Hardball." *Newsweek*, December 20, 2004, 52.

Book

McCloskey, John, and Julian Bailes. *When Winning Costs Too Much: Steroids, Supplements, and Scandal in Today's Sports*. Lanham, MD: Taylor Trade Publishing, 2005.

*All Web sites on these pages active at time of publication

Educational Slide Show

Partnership for a Drug-Free America and Major League Baseball Charities. "Sports Are Great—Steroids Aren't." Steroids facts and sports slide show. www.drugfree.org/Portal/Steroids/slideshow.html

Educational Videos and Brochures

National Federation of State High School Associations. *Make the Right Choice.* www.nfhs.org/web/2006/09/nfhs_steroids_awareness.aspx

HUMAN GROWTH HORMONE

Web Site

Ontario Genomics Institute. Information on growth hormone.
www.ontariogenomics.ca/education/episode5.asp

GENE DOPING

Article

Sweeney, H. Lee. "Gene Doping." *Scientific American*, July 2004, 62–69.
www.sciam.com/article.cfm?articleID=000E7ACE-5686-10CF-94EB83414B7F0000

CHILDREN'S HEALTH AND FITNESS

Web Site

The Nemours Foundation's Center for Children's Health Media.
KidsHealth for Parents. kidshealth.org/parent

Index

Amgen, 16, 17, 31, 33–34

anabolic steroid, 13, 24, 35, 39, 49–50, 51, 52, 53

Anti-Doping Research, Inc., 21

"A" sample ("A" bottle), 27

biomarker, 50, 51

blood booster, 4, 13, 15, 16, 17, 24, 31, 35

blood samples, 23

"B" sample ("B" bottle), 27

Catlin, Don, 12, 20–21, 30, 33–34, 37–38, 39, 45–46, 50

cheater, cheating, cheats, 12, 13, 15, 17, 19, 20, 39, 42, 46–47, 50, 52, 53

chemotherapy, 17

chromatography, 39, 51

corticosteroid, 35, 47, 51

Danilova, Olga, 42, 46–47

designer drug, 39, 51

DMT, 49

DNA. See recombinant DNA technology

doping, 9, 11–12, 13, 20–21, 29, 33, 37, 39, 43, 45, 49–50, 51, 52, 53, 54

Douglas, Zachary, 45–46

DSHEA, 49–50

Elliott, Steven, 16, 30, 31, 33–34, 37, 46

EPO, 15, 17, 24–25, 31, 33–34, 35, 41, 51, 52

EPO test, 24–25, 34

erythrocyte, 15

gel, 25, 34

gene doping, 49, 54

Gorzek, Jeff, 4, 12, 24–25, 42

hormone, 15, 17, 31, 35, 39, 49–50, 51, 54

human growth hormone, 49, 54

IOC (International Olympic Committee), 19, 29, 33, 34, 37–38, 41–42, 43, 45–46, 51

isoelectric focusing, 25

Lasne, Françoise, 24

Lazutina, Larissa, 42, 46

madol, 49

mass spectrometry, 39, 51

Minor League Baseball, 21

Muehlegg, Johann, 42

NCAA (National Collegiate Athletic Association), 21

NFL (National Football League), 21

NESP, 4, 16–17, 25–26, 28, 29–30, 31, 33–34, 37, 41–42, 45–47, 51

Olympics, ancient, 13

Olympics, modern, 13

Olympics, 1968 Mexico City, 16

Olympics, 1984 Los Angeles, 18, 19, 20, 41

Olympics, 1996 Atlanta, 19, 41

Olympics, 2000 Sydney, 43

Olympics, 2002 Salt Lake City, 8, 9, 10, 11, 16–17, 19, 22, 23, 24, 36, 40, 42

Olympics, 2004 Athens, 43

Paulsson, Jan, 45–46

pseudoephedrine, 43, 52

Raducan, Andreea, 43

recombinant DNA technology, 17, 31, 52

recombinant EPO, 15, 17, 25, 28, 33, 34, 52

red (blood) cell, 14, 15, 17, 51, 52

Rogge, Jacques, 37–38

RSR-13, 49

Scott, Beckie, 44, 46–47

Steroid Control Act, 49, 50

stimulant, 13, 24, 35, 43, 51, 52

strict liability, 43, 52

testosterone, 35, 39, 52

THG, 39, 49, 52

toxicity, 52

TUE (Therapeutic Use Exemption), 47, 52

UCLA (University of California at Los Angeles), 4, 12, 19, 20–21, 39

U.S. Olympic Committee, 21

Volunteer Program, 50

WADA (World Anti-Doping Agency), 21, 43, 47, 52, 53

Wash, Chris, 35

White, Kelli, 35

Picture Credits

BEREG-Kit, Courtesy of **Berlinger Special AG**: 27.

Bongarts/Getty Images: 38.

Joan Charles: 28.

CMS/Newscom: 14.

Sam Kleinman/**CORBIS**, front cover and jacket.

Jeff Gorzek: 34.

Caroline Hatton: 12 (top), 16, 24 (top and bottom), 25, 26, 30, 46 (bottom).

Lajla Hirsl: 8.

IOC/Giulio Locatelli: 32, 36, 44; Yo Nagaya: 3, 10, 22, 40, 42.

LA84 Foundation: 18.

REUTERS/Lyle Stafford: 46 (top).

Sanja H. Starcevic: 12 (bottom).

Time & Life Pictures/Getty Images: 13.

Jeff Minton, Courtesy of **UCLA Olympic Lab**: 20.

Michael Yarish: 21, back cover and jacket.